Thank you

THE C. R. GIBSON COMPANY, NORWALK, CONNECTICUT

Thank
You
These two words…"Thank You"…are too small to express my gratitude for your kindnesses.

You give so many gifts to others and not all of these are wrapped and tied with brightly colored ribbons. You give gentle words and thoughtful deeds, smiles that quickly spread to other faces, a quiet understanding of other's needs, a willingness to help in any way you can.

You probably think of your gifts as "little things," given without a thought of praise and soon forgotten. But the recipients of your goodness never forget. The memory of your kindnesses live on in so many hearts.

So, with my thank-you, comes this book of happy thoughts. I want to share them with you. And I hope that, at least in some small measure, they bring you the kind of happiness you always bring to others. Especially to me.

Love. Lou & Dick

Happiness Is a Gift

Above all, and this seems quite apparent to me, it is impossible to be happy if one does not have the desire to be happy; one must therefore will one's happiness, and create it.

What has not been sufficiently stressed is that we also have an obligation toward others to be happy. It is often said that only the happy are loved; but it is forgotten that this recompense is just and deserved; for unhappiness, boredom, and despair are in the air we all breathe; and so we owe thanks and a laurel wreath to those who dissipate the miasmas and, in a sense, purify life around us with their energetic example. There is indeed nothing more profound in love than the vow to be happy. What can be more difficult to overcome than the boredom, sadness, or unhappiness of those we love? Every man and every woman should always keep in mind the fact that happiness—I mean the happiness one conquers for oneself—is the most beautiful and the most generous gift one can give.

Alain

My Treasures

Nothing can erase the lovely things
    my life has known;
These treasures I shall always
    cherish as my very own.
The disappointments, unkind things,
    that have but touched my way
I brush aside, and quickly think
    upon the beauty of the day.
For each dawn brings a wonder
    I have not seen before,
And with that wonder comes the opening
    of still another door.
The blooming of a flower,
    the sunlight of the sea,
The kindness of a friend...
    all these are joys to me.

Marcella E. Minard

Little Things

Count

Half the joy of life is in little things taken on the run. Let us run if we must—even the sands do that—but let us keep our hearts young and our eyes open that nothing worth our while shall escape us. And everything is worth its while if we only grasp it and its significance.

Victor Cherbuliez

I'm Glad

The south wind is driving
His splendid cloud-horses
Through vast fields of blue.
The bare woods are singing,
The brooks in their courses
Are bubbling and springing,
And dancing and leaping,
The violets peeping,
I'm glad to be living:
    Aren't you?

               Gamaliel Bradford

Happy Times

The big events are too few and far between and frequently, when they do come, are disappointing. What makes life full, rich and worthwhile are the small happenings: gathering pecans with the children on a brisk fall afternoon; setting out tomato plants in the moist spring; riding the bus to town with a gossipy driver; showing friends the pale pink peonies and deep blue iris blooming simultaneously as they should...

Willie Snow Ethridge

Because of a Friend...

Because of a friend, life is a little stronger, fuller, more gracious thing for the friend's existence, whether he be near or far. If the friend is close at hand, that is best; but if he is far away he still is there to think of, to wonder about, to hear from, to write to, to share life and experience with, to serve, to honor, to admire, to love.

Arthur C. Benson

To A Friend

Because you are my friend
I long today
To bring you some imperishable gift
Of beauty:

Something glowing and warm
Like the coals of living fire,
Something as cool and sweet
As blue lilies at dawn,
Something as restful and clean
As smooth white sheets at night
When one is very tired,
Something with the taste of spring water
From high places,
Or like the tang of cool purple grapes
To the mouth.

But O my friend,
Since I cannot buy such gifts for you,
Come go with me
Out into the little everyday fields of living,
And let us gather in our baskets, like
        manna,
God's gift to us:

The down-pouring, exquisite beauty
Of life itself!

Grace Noll Crowell

Enjoying Life

When you wake up in the morning, you must alert yourself to the day ahead, to the possibilities for joyful living that the coming hours will bring—if you use them fully! The things you do during the day may not shake the world, but they may make your world.

Maxwell Maltz, M.D.

The day that goes by without your having had some fun—the day you don't enjoy life—is not only unnecessary but unchristian!

Dwight D. Eisenhower

The Vision of Beauty

A child's world is fresh and new and beautiful, full of wonder and excitement. It is our misfortune that for most of us that clear-eyed vision, that true instinct for what is beautiful and awe-inspiring, is dimmed and even lost before we reach adulthood.

Rachel Carson

The longer I live the more beautiful life becomes. The earth's beauty grows on men. If you foolishly ignore beauty, you'll soon find yourself without it. Your life will be impoverished. But if you wisely invest in beauty, it will remain with you all the days of your life.

Frank Lloyd Wright

Let's Have a Picnic

Let's have a picnic out-of-doors!
Let's make the beds, and do the chores,
Let's pack the basket high and take
The peach pie and the johnnycake,
And lemons, sugar, spoons, a cup:
Don't hesitate to fill it up.

Let's have a picnic out-of-doors!
We may not steam to foreign shores;
But to the meadow we can take
Our peach pie and our johnnycake,
And see the birds and trees—and eat,
And find existence there quite sweet.

Mary Carolyn Davies

Joy I suppose it all started when Ethan was born...As I looked at him, he was very quiet and very curious. He lay quite still, concentrating on the "blooming, buzzing confusion," apparently entranced. For an hour we held him, and he was warm and close and peaceful. I even found myself trying to explain what he was getting into—and he listened carefully. I kept thinking that this might be the most important hour of his life. What a way to begin, by giving joy to parents!

The joy continues. When Ethan smiles, every cell of his body smiles, including his turned-up toes. When he is unhappy, he is thoroughly unhappy, all over. When he is interested in a new object, only he and the object exist. He touches it, tastes it, smells it, puts it in things, puts things in it, gives it to people, takes it from people, looks at it from far and from near. The total absorption is beautiful to watch.

And his pleasure now, during his first fifteen months, is mainly physical—being thrown up in the air, sliding off the refrigerator into his father's arms, being tickled and hugged, having his cheeks chewed, his behind munched, his face caressed, rubbing his cheek against another's cheek. And he touches. It's hard to match the feeling of his little finger exploring my teeth way inside my mouth while his face has that curious, intent look.

And on it goes. He is joyful and he gives joy. He wakes up each morning eager for new adventure. Maybe today it will be a piece of string, or the toilet plunger, or the telephone, or pots and pans, or—more rarely—a new toy.

Ethan is joy. He enjoys each aspect of his life with his whole being. He gives joy to those near him. His joy is contagious.

William C. Schutz

The Enjoyment of Beauty

I watched the little girl as she ran down the street. She was a dirty, ragged child with unkempt, half-braided hair flying. She stopped abruptly at the sight of my neighbor's bed of brilliant, prize tulips.

The child seemed spellbound at the sight of such beauty. Then, bending slightly, she reached out her hand. I caught my breath—she was going to pull the flowers!

But she didn't. Instead, she leaned forward and, choosing the largest one, she patted it lovingly and tenderly as if it were a puppy.

Turning, she sped away at top speed. That little girl, I thought, knew something many people never learn—the sheer enjoyment of beauty is sufficient pleasure—one need not possess to appreciate.

Anna Smith

Altar Smoke

Somewhere inside of me
There must have always been
A tenderness
For the little, lived-with things
A man crowds upon his worn fistful of earth.
Somewhere inside of me
There must have always been
A love
Made to fill the square aggressiveness of
    new-cut hedges,
And feed the pursed green mouths of baby
    leaves;
A love made to understand
The way grass cuddles up to porch steps
    leaned upon by time,
And why dandelions nudge the stones
    along the walk;
A love for garden hose curled sleeping in
    the noon hush,
Coolness trickling lazily from its open mouth,
For shingles starched and saucy in white
    paint,
And an old rake rusty with dreams of tan-
    gled grass and butterflies.
A love
For candle flames, like pointed blossoms on
    their ghostly stems,
And frost-forests breathing wonder on the
    parlor windows.

Somewhere inside of me
There must have always been
An altar of hewn stones
Upon which my love casts these—
Burnt offerings—
To make a sweet savor
Unto my soul.

Give me the strength, my God,
To scatter my fires and tumble the altar
        stones in confusion;
Give me the strength to raise my eyes,
So that hard and sharp across my heart
Like shadow cut on mountain rock,
Will fall the agony of sunset—
So that I can see
The laughter of clouds spun into the blue
        web of infinity,
So that my soul can reach out
And melt in the sweep of forever
Above all these.

Rosalie Grayer

Smells

Why is it that the poets tell
So little of the sense of smell?
These are the odors I love well:

The smell of coffee freshly ground;
Or rich plum pudding, holly-crowned;
Or onions fried and deeply browned.

The fragrance of a fumy pipe;
The smell of apples, newly ripe;
And printer's ink on leaden type.

Woods by moonlight in September
Breathe most sweet; and I remember
Many a smoky campfire ember.

Camphor, turpentine, and tea,
The balsam of a Christmas tree,
These are whiffs of gramarye...
A ship smells best of all to me!

Christopher Morley

Sounds

One does not live in vain to have heard
    the birds' songs in spring,
    the cicadas' songs in summer,
    the insects' chirps in autumn, and
    the sounds of crunching snow in winter,
and furthermore, to have heard
    the sound of chess in daytime,
    the sound of flute in moonlight,
    the sound of winds whistling through
      the pines,
      and
    the sound of rippling, lapping water.

Chang Chao

Laughter
It dawned on me then that as long as I could laugh, I was safe from the world; and I have learned since that laughter keeps me safe from myself, too. All of us have schnozzles—are ridiculous in one way or another, if not in our faces, then in our characters, minds or habits. When we admit our schnozzles, instead of defending them, we begin to laugh, and the world laughs with us.

Jimmy Durante

Strange, when you come to think of it, that of all countless folk who have lived on this planet not one is known in history or in legend as having died of laughter.

Sir Max Beerbohm

Conversation never sits easier than when we now and then discharge ourselves in a symphony of laughter; which may not improperly be called the chorus of conversation.

Sir Richard Steele

Life pays a bonus to those who learn that laughter is a vital part of living. It is one of God's richest gifts. The Lord loves a cheerful giver; but He also loves the cheerful—period. And so does everyone else.

Edwin Davis

I live in a constant endeavor to fence against the infirmities of ill-health, and other evils of life, by mirth. I am persuaded that every time a man smiles—but much more so when he laughs—it adds something to this fragment of life.

Laurence Sterne

Sharing
Happiness

Joy is contagious. It can spread like wildfire
and wipe the worry from people's minds
and keep your thoughts ready for positive
action.

Quiet happiness is also catching, when
a person quietly gives another enjoyment he
makes the other person glad he's alive. He
turns worry to joy and hate to love.

Maxwell Maltz, M.D.

Little gifts keep friendship green.

Montesquieu

For life alone is creator of life,
And closest contact with the human world
Is like a lantern shining in the night
To light me to a knowledge of myself.

Amy Lowell

A kind heart is a fountain of gladness, making everything in its vicinity freshen into smiles.

Washington Irving

The Ever Open Door

What shall I bestow upon a friend? Gay laughter to sustain him when sorrow may bring pain? A bright song of life, belief that winter ends in the glory of spring, a prayer of hope for peace that will ever stay.

What shall I bestow upon a friend? Songs from my heart which I've hidden away? Friendship that flowers, once it enters the heart, spring's eternal loveliness, knowledge that love is a precious thing.

What shall I bestow upon a friend? Fleeting moments of silent blessings? Trust in tomorrow, which is life's hardest task, faith that each new dawn brings daylight's golden pathways to the ever-open door, belief that God will be with him though all others go their way.

Lea Palmer

Live!

Come clean with a child heart
Laugh as peaches in the summer wind.
Let rain on a house-roof be a song.
Let the writing on your face be a smell
     of apple orchards in late June.

Carl Sandburg

The Good
Life

Friendships, family ties, the companionship of little children, an autumn forest flung in prodigality against a deep blue sky, the intricate design and haunting fragrance of a flower, the counterpoint of a Bach fugue or the melodic line of a Beethoven sonata, the fluted note of bird song, the glowing glory of a sunset: the world is aflame with things of eternal moment.

E. Margaret Clarkson

And in the sweetness of friendship let there be laughter, and sharing of pleasures.
For in the dew of little things the heart finds its morning and is refreshed.

Kahlil Gibran

What sunshine is to flowers, smiles are to humanity. They are but trifles, but scattered along life's pathway the good they do is inconceivable.

Joseph Addison

There is an emanation from the heart in genuine hospitality which cannot be described, but is immediately felt and puts the stranger at once at his ease.

Washington Irving

Nothing on earth can smile but man. Gems may flash reflected-light, but what is a diamond-flash compared to an eye-flash and a mirth-flash? Flowers cannot smile; this is a charm that even they cannot claim. It is the prerogative of man; it is the color which love wears, and cheerfulness, and joy—these three. It is a light in the windows of the face by which the heart signifies it is at home and waiting. A face that cannot smile is like a bud that cannot blossom, and dries up on the stalk. Laughter is day, and sobriety is night, and a smile is the twilight that hovers gently between both—more bewitching than either.

Henry Ward Beecher

This world, after all our science and sciences, is still a miracle; wonderful, inscrutable, magical and more, to whosoever will think of it.

Thomas Carlyle

Invasions
of Beauty

Experiences of beauty steal up swiftly on us
and take us over for the moment.
A clump of wild pink lady's-slippers deep in
the wood;
the song of the hermit thrush at dusk;
a marshy bank of a brook ablaze with cardi-
nal flowers;
an opening in the veil of "thundering
smoke" and the flash of the mighty
Zambezi majestically hurling itself into
its chasm at Victoria Falls;
the sight of a lone column of a Greek temple
standing sentinel on the deserted Sici-
lian plain at Segesta;
a sonnet of Shakespeare's;
a line of Gerard Manley Hopkins such as
"Glory be to God for dappled things";
a fugue of Bach's;
a Van Gogh sunflower—
and the curtain to the inner stage has lifted.
These invasions of beauty may be rung
down at once, or the lights to the stage
may fade gradually, but after such
openings, a man is not the same and
the memory may shed its fragrance over
all that follows.

Douglas V. Steere

Miracles

There is no such thing as an average man. Each one of us is a unique individual. Each one of us expresses his humanity in some distinctly different way. The beauty and the bloom of each human soul is a thing apart—a separate holy miracle under God, never once repeated throughout all the millenniums of time.

Lane Weston

There are some people who have the quality of richness and joy in them and they communicate it to everything they touch. It is first of all a physical quality; then it is a quality of the spirit.

Thomas Wolfe

Liking
Brings
Rewards

Liking people is one of the important ingredients for getting the most out of life. If you like people, you have a zest, an enthusiasm for working and for living—you give of yourself to others and, in return, you find yourself getting a great deal from them. Once it becomes a part of you it will pay dividends not only in your work but in sheer enjoyment of living.

Samuel Goldwyn

Now Is the Time to Rejoice

"This is the day which the Lord hath made." We shall never overtake tomorrow. Wherever we are, it will always be today. So if ever we are to be glad we are alive, and relaxed in a childlike gala mood of appreciation for all the things we have to enjoy, and of gratitude to their Giver, now is the time to begin. "This is the day which the Lord hath made; we will rejoice and be glad in it." That is common sense. And, even if we try, we cannot fret and worry at the same time we are rejoicing and being glad.

Russell Henry Stafford

I find that nonsense, at times, is singularly refreshing.

Charles Maurice de Talleyrand-Périgord

A characteristic of the great saints is their power of levity. Angels can fly because they take themselves lightly. One "settles down" into a sort of selfish seriousness; but one has to rise to a gay self-forgetfulness. A man falls into a "brown study"; he reaches up at a blue sky.

Gilbert Keith Chesterton

A bookworm in bed with a new novel and a good reading lamp is as much prepared for pleasure as a pretty girl at a college dance.

Phyllis McGinley

Who's In

"The door is shut fast
And everyone's out."
But people don't know
What they are talking about!

Says the fly on the wall,
And the flame on the coals,
And the dog on his rug,
And the mice in their holes,
And the kitten curled up,
And the spiders that spin—
"What, everyone out?
Why, everyone's in!"

Elizabeth Fleming

Counters

To think I once saw grocery shops
With but a casual eye
And fingered figs and apricots
As one who came to buy!

To think I never dreamed of how
Bananas swayed in rain,
And often looked at oranges
Yet never thought of Spain!

And in those wasted days I saw
No sails above the tea—
For grocery shops were grocery shops,
Not hemispheres to me!

Elizabeth Coatsworth

The gayety of life, like the beauty and the moral worth of life, is a saving grace, which to ignore is folly, and to destroy is crime. There is no more than we need—there is barely enough to go round.

Agnes Repplier

True humor springs not more from the head than from the heart. It is not contempt; its essence is love. It issues not in laughter, but in still smiles, which lie far deeper.

Thomas Carlyle

Honest good humor is the oil and wine of a merry meeting, and there is no jovial companionship equal to that where the jokes are rather small, and the laughter abundant.

Washington Irving

An inexhaustible good nature is one of the
most precious gifts of heaven, spreading itself like oil over the troubled sea of thought,
and keeping the mind smooth and equable
in the roughest weather.

Washington Irving

For health and the constant enjoyment of
life, give me a keen and ever present sense
of humor; it is the next best thing to an abid-
ing faith in providence.

George Barrell Cheever

To see things as they are, the eyes must be
open; to see things as other than they are,
they must open even wider; to see things as
better than they are, they must be open to
the full.

Antonio Machado

Sunbeams of Warmth

The hands of those I meet are eloquent to me. I have met people so empty of joy that when I clasped their frosty fingertips it seemed as if I were shaking hands with a northeast storm. Others there are whose hands have sunbeams in them, so that their grasp warms my heart. It may be only the clinging touch of a child's hand, but there is as much potential sunshine in it for me as there is in a loving glance for others.

Helen Keller

Miracles

Why, who makes much of a miracle?
As to me I know of nothing else but miracles,
Whether I walk the streets of Manhattan,
Or dart my sight over the roofs of houses
    toward the sky,
Or wade with naked feet along the beach
    just in the edge of the water,
Or stand under trees in the woods,
Or sit at table at dinner with the rest,
Or look at strangers opposite me riding in
    the car,
Or watch honey-bees busy around the hive
    of a summer forenoon,
Or animals feeding in the fields,
Or birds, or the wonderfulness of insects in
    the air,
Or the wonderfulness of the sundown, or of
    stars shining so quiet and bright,
Or the exquisite delicate thin curve of the
    new moon in spring;
These with the rest, one and all, are to me
    miracles,

The whole referring, yet each distinct and in
    its place.

To me every hour of the light and dark is a
    miracle,
Every cubic inch of space is a miracle,
Every square yard of the surface of the
    earth is spread with the same,
Every foot of the interior swarms with the
    same.

To me the sea is a continual miracle,
The fishes that swim—the rocks—the motion
    of the waves—the ships with men in
    them,
What stranger miracles are there?
                                    Walt Whitman

Thank You

All day long a blackbird sang. All day long
the garden rang—with notes that fell like
silver spray—on the lilac and the may...Was
it just a common bird—made the music that I
heard—or did angels hovering, teach the
blackbird how to sing—and human beings
how to say—Thank you for a lovely day?

Patience Strong

Acknowledgments

The editor and the publisher have made every effort to trace the ownership of all copyrighted material and to secure permission from copyright holders of such material. In the event of any question arising as to the use of any material the publisher and editor, while expressing regret for inadvertent error, will be pleased to make the necessary corrections in future printings. Thanks are due to the following authors, publishers, publications and agents for permission to use the material indicated.

COWARD, MCCANN & GEOGHEGAN, INC., for "Counters" from *Compass Rose* by Elizabeth Coatsworth, copyright 1929 by Coward-McCann, Inc., renewed 1957 by Elizabeth Coatsworth.

RUPERT CREW LIMITED, for "Thank You" by Patience Strong.

ELIZABETH FLEMING, for "Who's In?"

GROVE PRESS, INC., for excerpt from "Joy Expanding" from *Human Awareness* by William C. Schutz, copyright © 1967 by William C. Schutz.

Harper & Row, Publishers, Inc., for excerpt from *The Sense of Wonder* by Rachel Carson, copyright © 1956 by Rachel L. Carson; for "To A Friend" from *Some Brighter Dawn* by Grace Noll Crowell, copyright 1943 by Harper & Row, Publishers, Inc.; for "Invasions of Beauty" from *Work and Contemplation* by Douglas V. Steere, copyright © 1957 by Douglas V. Steere.

HARCOURT BRACE JOVANOVICH, INC., for excerpt from "Lesson" from *Honey and Salt* by Carl Sandburg, copyright © 1963 by Carl Sandburg.

HOUGHTON MIFFLIN COMPANY, for excerpt from "Summer" from *The Complete Works of Amy Lowell*.

ALFRED A. KNOPF, INC., for excerpt from *The Prophet* by Kahlil Gibran, copyright 1923 by Kahlil Gibran, renewed 1951 by Administrators C.T.A. of Kahlil Gibran Estate and Mary G. Gibran.

J. B. LIPPINCOTT COMPANY, for "Smells" from *The Rocking Horse* by Christopher Morley, copyright 1919, renewed 1947 by Christopher Morley.

LEA PALMER, for "The Ever Open Door."

FREDERICK UNGAR PUBLISHING CO. INC., for excerpt from *Alain On Happiness*, copyright © 1973 by Frederick Ungar Publishing Co. Inc.

Selected by Elizabeth Gibson

Set in Stymie Light
Designed by Bonnie Havada

Photo Credits